Milepost 27
Poems

BOOKS BY MARILYN STABLEIN

Poetry

Milepost 27
Splitting Hard Ground
Night Travels to Tibet
More Night Travels to Tibet

Fiction

Vermin: A Bestiary
The Census Taker: Tales of a Traveler in India and Nepal
The Monkey Thief

Nonfiction

Houseboat on the Ganges & A Room in Kathmandu
Sleeping in Caves: A Sixties Himalayan Memoir
Climate of Extremes: Landscape and Imagination

Art

Bind,Alter, Fold: Artist Books

Limited Editions

Phantom Circus
A Pot of Soup
High in the Himalayas
Intrusions in Ice
Ticketless Traveler

Milepost 27
Poems

Marilyn Stablein

*For John
new Mexico's
finest!
Best
Marilyn*

Marilyn Stablein

Black Heron Press
Post Office Box 13396
Mill Creek, Washington 98082
www.blackheronpress.com

A number of the poems, some in earlier versions, originally appeared in the following publications: *Afterthought*: "Perfect Rice;" *Central Avenue*: "Inventory;" *Duke City Fix*: "Poet's Couch;" *Fresh Hot Bread*: "Ticklers;" *Malpais Review*: "Hungry Ghosts," "Live from the Uptown," "Effigy," "Roadside Attraction," "What's to Love in a Porcupine," "Reconnaissance," "Jornada del Muerto," "Blue Alchemy;" *Mas Tequila Review*: "Bone Altar;" *New Mexico Poetry Review*: "How to Build a Descanso;" *Otoliths*: "Sacred Fire," "Tibetan New Year;" *PostPoem Number Nine*: "Bone Black;" *Santa Fe Literary Review*: "Seduction by Soap;" *The Arts*: "Anklet," "Heat Wave," "You Come Bearing Gifts;" *Windfall*: "Rosario Strait;" *THE Magazine*: "Pyro City;"*Cascadia*: "Niagara;" *Catalyst Anthology*: "To Keep the Cold Out;" *Harwood Anthology*: "Weeds, Tended or Not;" *Honoring Our Rivers*: "Cannery Pier;" *La Llorona Anthology*: "Bereaved;" *Make It True*: *Poetry from Cascadia*: "Above, Below Ground;" "What Water Carries."

The author is grateful the New Mexico Press Women selected "How to Build a Descanso" for the 2012 poetry prize.

ISBN: 978-1-936364-31-2

Black Heron Press
Post Office Box 13396
Mill Creek, Washington 98082
www.blackheronpress.com

CONTENTS

ONE

NIAGARA

Mark the trails.
Who or what leads?
Trampled ground
maps a route.

A steep climb
slows the pace.
Labored breath,
the drudgery of ascent.

Is progress
measured by arrival
or the anticipation
of return?

Missing you
my heart trails.
Like water losing
the ground

it glides over
the rush, the drop
crushes a ragged
trail through grief.

COMPASS

The heart measures
without ruler or yardstick.
No meter, dial or glass scope.
Eyes skyward track, gauge

clouds, their formations
and shifts. The higher the altitude
the greater the horizon.
When the mountain blew

itself inside out, distant
puffing umbrella cloud
plumed a hundred fifty
miles to the south. Puzzled,

I waded Alki's gentle waves.
Explosives? Geyser? Reactor?
I never saw before or will again
a lava dome sculpt the stratosphere.

TWO

WHAT WATER CARRIES

Off shore row boat bucks
wind-whitened caps, roiling
lightning-charged waves.
Lines of salmon trollers
hem the broad Columbia. Poetics
of motion across vast space.

Memory veers
like a tidal river, doubles back,
whirls eddy-like in reverse.
No straight path between
points, thoughts, and
the litany of associations.

In Kashmir downstream
from Shiva's swollen full
moon frozen phallus in cloistered
Amarnath cave, frigid glacial
ice melt numbed my fingers
busy scouring charred rice pot

with a palm full of ash.
When walking high desert
sand banks through sparse
salt cedar forest, sandals
rub like sandpaper. Naked soles
raw. Soothing then

to wade warm waters,
dislodge gritty sand. Across
millennia draining, snaking river
whittles granite cliffs. Abrasive,
grit-muddled water chisels bedrock,
sculpts terraced canyon gorge.

ROSARIO STRAIT

"A dollar if you see
an Orca," I say,
a lure or bribe to keep
restless son's eyes

focused on choppy
San Juan waters.
To peer as a sailor
might skim the horizon

each dawn scouting
treacherous swells,
slow-moving black clouds.
Open poetry book splayed

across my lap, island
reveries of favorite fresh
water swimming holes.
"You owe me!" Willie

interrupts. "Two dollars!"
Out the ferry window
dulled from countless
salty wind-sprayed

blasts, he points.
Gracefully gliding up,
over bumpy wave crests
not one but two Orcas

play ferry tag
leap, race in tandem.

CANNERY PIER

Sand bars stretch five miles
across Columbia's gaping maw.
Sea lions navigate treacherous
shoals, gorge on sockeye,
chinook and coho.

Largest salmon run since
the Bonneville barricaded
ancient ancestral waterway.
Redolent, satiated intruders
cram every inch of rickety

marina dock near Cannery Pier
where we grip coffee mugs
tight, inhale luscious steam,
strong brew. Ceaseless lapping
waves below rock the deck.

Streamlined whiskered snout
breaks the water's surface.
Envious newcomer surveys
the crowd. Satisfied, he hooks
front flippers on wood ledge

launches bulging hefty
body atop the others.
A chorus of mock
raucous grousing
as one more barges in.

Packed tight as sardines,
a child's game we played
squeezed together in cramped
hideout. Lone seeker counted
aloud: *Ready or Not! Here I Come!*

Loud barks audible
a mile uphill. What do
they yelp about?
The great feast?
Smaller anchovy run?

Rising waters? Warmer
temperatures? On and on
late into, through the night.
Barks jar the dreaming
mind's ferment, night sweats.

SEA MARCH

Lemmings cluster in a colony deep
in a coastal cliff. In time they emerge
en masse, scurry like soldiers
to a battlefield, travel as the crow flies.

Hundreds join the march. Neither house
nor creek, road nor lake impedes progress.
Unarmed, they do not fight each other
or enemies along the way. Wanderlust

has no schedule, no fixed destination.
Their journey is not a protest or political
statement. The sea rises, siren-like,
an immense obstacle or distraction.

Theories abound: the young abandon
home to ease overcrowding; the sick to
protect the healthy. That glorious airborne
lunge—running leap, arms, legs spread

wide to freefall like a flying squirrel,
plunge in a choppy sea. They tread
water but frigid weather limits stamina.
Without rest, food or sleep scores drown.

How many wash ashore, swim
to uncharted lands, catch rides
on dolphins' backs? Or settle down
like Jonah, keep house in a whale's belly?

WHAT'S TO LOVE IN A PORCUPINE

One morning before dawn's
cool waning night, I yank
tenacious bag worms off plum,
apricot leaves. In fertile, amenable
seasons ripe fruits to harvest.

A tough year, killer frost,
summer drought. Now worms
pick the branches clean like
ants suck carcass bones dry.
Sudden movement—

ten feet away furtive creature
waddles past. Proud, not wimpy,
tough not shy. No hurry,
not aggressive yet formidable
to behold. I step back.

Projecting skin-piercing quills—
that's a myth but neighbor's vicious
dog reaped a snoutful of spears only
a vet could extract. Piercing
yowls, goose-bumped skin.

A male's dilemma: how to
court a spear-armed mate?
Not by force. The female picks

the time and place to rest her
quills, let a lover near.
Independence, the power of choice.

ALAMOCITOS

Solstice ritual
winter pilgrimage
I journey hundreds of miles

to simmer chilled bones
in scalding Geronimo
springs. Night sweats bathe

restless limbs. Steam-pool
bubbles tickle callused
soles. Ten thousand voices,

restless river, owl's haunted
hoots. Early Spanish explorers
camped by sacred

springs at Alamocitos
where little cottonwoods
still thrive. No walls, fences

or skin puncturing barbs
kept bathers out. No money
changed hands. Apache warriors,

sworn enemies, shared
thermal springs, soothed battle
wounds, bitter hearts.

HUNGRY GHOSTS

for Todd Moore

Deer grass claws
a Montauk shore.
Under pant legs
ticks like thorny stickers
puncture the skin.
Raw shills
pummel
the naked spine.

Thirsting vampires
hijack the mind. Words
like blood on Kali's
drooling tongue.
Outlaw denizens
of a lusting,
pitiful hell.

Twist and pull,
one at a time.
Check between
toes. Scalp,
dark crevices
ticks love most.

Blood thicker
than ink in the vein.
Fever-carrying

hungry ghosts
suck into our lives
tapping the blood line,
vacuuming
under the skin.

THE BOOK OF SOAP

The French poet Francis Ponge obsessed
about ordinary things: a candle, the stove,
the telephone. He wrote an entire book on
soap. Did a scarcity during the Resistance
fuel fascination with that scented bar?

In the fifties father on out-of-town
business trips packed in his suitcase
small rectangular bars wrapped in white
paper embossed with names like
Winnemucca Roadside Inn and

Bakersfield Travel Lodge. His stack
in the bathroom medicine cabinet
reached ten inches then slowly
diminished as he conscientiously
used the soap up one at a time.

One Christmas I gave him a cologne
soap to hang by a rope in his shower.
Nana hung a soap strainer in her pantry.
To save a dime she hoarded soap ends
to melt then molded a fresh bar

to use for her weekly bath.
During and after the great depression
survivors despised wastefulness,
like the woman at the yard sale
who put a dollar price tag

on a scruffy candy box filled
with dozens of spent soap ends.
"I can't throw them out," she confessed,
imagining a market for her used
lavender, pine and sandalwood bath chips.

CARTOGRAPHY OF CURES

To heal aching bones
        soak in the mud
        baths of Calistoga

To energize sluggish limbs
        dip in Ojo Caliente's
        mineral rich waters

To cleanse the intestines
        eat clay dirt, what
        the Greeks call *geoghagia*

For a natural sunscreen
        dust like an elephant, toss
        powdered dirt over heat sensitive skin

To rid hair of lice
        rub fine ashen powder into
        the scalp to suffocate vermin

To abide grief
        walk the tidal shores
        of the heart's reservoir

For the pious
        smear ash paste over skin like
        the naked *nagababas* of Hindustan

SEDUCTION BY SOAP

Last week at Ojo hot springs
I slathered handfuls of soupy adobe
mud over my body till only my teeth
and the whites of my eyes gleamed

like a sooty coal monger
in a Dickens novel. The wind
buffeted; my earth-caked
skin cracked like a drought-

parched river bed. Once moss
and seaweed scrubbed,
cleansed. When I bathed in
the Ganga at Varanasi,

water laced with cremation
pyre ash toned my skin. Ash
scoured my aluminum rice pot
better than a sudsy steel wool pad.

How luxurious a bar of soap.
Beyond cleanliness and thrift,
lovers share the seductions of soap.
Hotel room tryst in a strange city,

love all afternoon, then sudsing
each other's amazing, love-worn
body in a brimming
bubble-filled tub.

THREE

RECONNAISSANCE

From the plane above Chichuahuan
yucca stands and fire barrel cactus
I site the Rio Grande whose grit
and brimstone waters like a primordial

grinding stone sandblasts over time
rift valley clefts, chisels deep scars
in ancient volcanic charnel ground.
Adobe, chili, Angel Fire, blood—

the ardor of fire's palette: scarlet, ruby,
maroon and agate. Red Mountain,
Red Rock, swollen muddy
Red River. What is the color of

Jornada del Muerto where Death's
long, hot tortuous trail charred
stone? Sinister badlands
void of greenery, petrified

moonscapes, skeletal
bone-porous pumice boulders—
a desert's incendiary history etched
in stone like a blowtorch cuts into steel.

EFFIGY

I

Each fall Zozobra, old man
gloom, writhes atop fifty foot
bonfire tower in Santa Fe,
the place of holy faith.

Long muslin sleeves erupt
in flames. Stick arms, hands sizzle,
pop. Paper mache mask ignites
the night. Expectant crowds witness

his public demise like those at
a witch hunt. But no martyr here.
Zozobra embodies sorrow,
anguish, trouble. Fire spirits

battle him. Dancers
celebrate the vanquished
foe. Call him Wicker Man,
Guy Fawkes: ritual scapegoat

flares, hisses, cackles. Diviners
cast herbs, salt temple hearths,
predict the morrow in curling
smoke, flaming whorls.

II

A week before Tibetan losar
a monk at Swayambhu gompa
in Kathmandu takes sculptor's chisel
to large black clay mound. Slowly
the monstrous head of Mahakala

inhabits inert mud: fanged snarl,
wrinkled nostrils, bulging fireball
sockets. Ferocious head crowned
with towering stick cubes. On top
a trapezoid gently wrapped
with rainbow threads.

The structure towers like a tent.
Pine torch ignites the effigy.
Twelve-foot, wind-whipped
flames cremate invisible demons
who writhe in tangled
spirit web like flies
on flypaper. A year's bad
karma up in smoke.

DESERT TOPOLOGY

With tattered road map
spread on my lap, I view
the desert from above
as if from a hot air balloon

or atop a raven's feathered
back. Shades of mesquite,
sand, saguaro mark vast
open spaces but black,

fire's legacy, names the arid
waste land of petrified lava
lakes: Black Mesa, Black
Canyon, Black Dome.

Lava beds stretch across
the Valley of Fires, circle
Black Top Mountain.
Rippled topographical lines

where fire bedded down,
smothered, crusted
desert floor like
a clay death mask.

ROADSIDE ATTRACTION

South side of Route 66
near Gallup, dilapidated
wood shack's sign:
LOUNGE & LIQUOR
flakes like dandruff
in late September sun.

We're stranded
waiting for a 50-mile tow.
No Uranium Café
or painted, frosted
air conditioned window
to lure bleary-eyed travelers.

Crumbling motor court
adobe wall embedded
with rusty hub caps.
Ghost trading posts,
weary sentinels,
the Cathedral peaks,

Chimney rocks
of a bypassed roadway.
In the beginning travelers
clogged four-lane
mother road, first
cross-country highway

to adventure, fun.
Bargains galore
at yellow-painted cement
wigwam shops perched
under red rock cliffs:
dream catcher trinkets,

striped Indian blankets.
CASH & CARRY
or PAWN & TRADE:
fetishes, beads, drums, belts.
Plan twenty miles ahead
for fry bread in Indian

City and 27 Modern Stations.
Later depression era
families, hungry,
out-of-work, begged
for gas gallon by gallon,
to carry them west

a mile at a time.
Ashen dust bowl
refugees traded leads
on seasonal work,
who's hiring, when, where.
Some stretches deadly,

accidents so common
locals branded the route
Camino de la Muerte,
Blood Alley. Like players
in a tattered, faded
Loteria Game

we wait for our luck
to change, watch
the Interstate for a tow truck
an hour after we call.
Two ravens covet
half-empty water bottle,

dried grapes, sunscreen,
peanuts. We'll be four,
five hours late if the car
is fixable. Overhead
intense relentless sun,
cloud-drained sky.

HOW TO BUILD A DESCANSO

Descanso, Spanish noun. 1. Rest, repose. 2. Stillness, tranquility. 3. A roadside memorial shrine.

I

In the dictionary *descanso* is a resting
place, a tranquil troubled shrine that
marks the beloved's sudden, irreversible
departure on some forlorn deserted road.

Like a hummingbird is attracted to crimson
flowers, when I travel the arroyos of the
grieved my eyes shelter in these shaggy altars
nestled between clumps of chamisa and sage.

Names of loved ones resting in memory, line
up to be counted. If you pass milepost 27
on the interstate look for my son's *descanso*.
At night I rebuild his shrine in my sleep.

II

Begin with the heart
whose ragged shards lie broken
like windshield glass on pavement.
In shattered bits fleeting glints of sun.

Breath comes next. Where the soul leapt
into memory and dream, breath catches.
Panting heart quickens, numbs. Whispered
prayers of angels beckon, soothe.

Bring mementos, love's amulets,
festive wreaths and tinsel. Nothing a thief
might steal, nothing rain, snow or wind
might ruin. Unbreakable flowers

without scent, photo in a frame, wooden
or tin cross. Disconsolate heart seeks
refuge in spinning wheels pinned on
prickly pear's blood-stained thorns.

BEREAVED

Every month parents who lost a child
come together. I was afraid at first.
What could I say to strangers?
Or they to me? Grief is personal,
deep and lasting. Still after ten years

when I try to mouth three simple words...
my... son... died... I break up. Lose it.
Tear-carved arroyos crisscross my
cheeks like facial scars of warriors.
To begin a moment of silence.

Soon thundering footsteps rattle
cupboard dishes. Angry woman
of the ditch banks, *la Llorona*, is a
regular here. People say she drowned
her children to be with a lover.

"I lost my children!" she enters, wailing.
Remorse drags like a rusty plow
through clay, a prisoner's ball on a chain.
Sleep-starved eyes shoot needles, knives.
"Are they here?" An Ophelia risen

from the creek's bed, her
murderous wails, keening
bellows through our bones.

BONE ALTAR

I pumped all over
going on seventeen years.
Yours is old, Ray, the septic
guy, says sticking the wide
nozzle down the dark hole.

Wonder what they found
digging this? Old Indian trail
ran right through here—
he motions where the acequia
flows behind the house.

Taos Indians migrated south,
followed the Rio Grande.
He stares off into the distance
as if he could see the river
beyond the cottonwoods.

They buried kin along the way.
Old Indian burial grounds
across the river.... That new adobe
mansion just before the Alameda
bridge? Right after it was built

owner died, heart attack.
Only forty-one.
Spirits weren't happy.
Another neighbor's dog
kept dragging in bones

41

he dug in the yard:
old, restless, sacred bones.
Husband built a special
bone room. Big brass
padlock on the door.

No one allowed in. Medicine
Man blessed the altar,
prayed over the land.
Didn't help. He died last
March. He was young, too.

PYRO CITY

Driving north to Nambe
flame-licked road signs
spell out fire's culinary treats.
Lov'n Oven Bakery's
hot bread aroma, Tewa
Smokehouse barbecued ribs.

String clusters of hanging
crimson sun-dried chili
ristras. Time to add sizzle,
charbroiled and roasted
to the dictionary of fire.
Think sauté, simmer, flambé.

Think incinerate, cremate,
inferno. Grungy Cinderella,
ash and cinder sweeper
and poor Hansel almost shoved
into the witch's oven cauldron.
From the poet's lexicon

inflamed and luminescence
leap to mind. The best
sign—Pyro City—an entire
warehouse tent
of Black Cat fire crackers,
rocket streamers,

blazers. Top of the line
year-around incendiary
sparklers, star bursts.
Roman candles,
cherry bombs, fire
wheels for every use.

Fire's contagious
airborne arc:
wrenching cannon shot,
thundering echo,
glorious ascension,
sky bursting brilliance,

rainbow sparks,
fountains. Cascading
withering spirals,
ghostly streaks
dying glow,
acrid ash.

SKY DROP

Lightning strikes torch
drought-stressed pines.
Winds lash, fan ravenous
flames. Ancient forests
reduced to black soot.

Rhythms lost to memory:
rain-bashed window panes,
hail-fracked windshields.
Catastrophic, dire,
calamitous—a surfeit

of demonic superlatives.
Fighters from Texas
to Utah, zero containment
in four, five, seven days.
Chopper raids shrunken

reservoir, dips, fills
bathtub-sized rubber
bucket. Precious water
dropped like a bomb,
vaporizes midair.

BEYOND MEASURE

When I trekked
the Himalayas north
of Darjeeling clustered
embers glowed in a trailside pit.
With a branch I stoked waning

coals. Cheeks flushed, palms
toasted. But suddenly I realized
—with a gasp--
wood didn't generate
such warmth. No pilgrim
camped here.

Abandoned to winds
cremation bones, porous
and delicate, glowed
in the cloud-soaked monsoon.

I pulled back as if I had touched
a leper or kissed a corpse
as I did in a dream—the moment
lips touched I gagged, horrified.

Like a recalcitrant dog
on a leash my eyes refused
to look away. Crystalline,
fire blushing trance—a body's
expiring bone-dispersing gasp.

I understood then
the regeneration of ash.
In fire's wake every
conceivable living, breathing
being reduced to the merest
particles. Charred powder,
pulverized dust.

More than deconstruction,
fire's devastation
exemplifies a democracy
so uniform the very nature
of disintegration
implies integration,
beyond measure,
form or doubt.

FOUR

PHANTOM FOREST

When oak and pine
logs smolder overnight
in the wood-burning stove
by morning what remains

is the tenuous cohesion
of ash, shaped like
the stumps fire consumed.
Twice logged, twice

burned, the ponderosa
forest above Jemez
survived the Dome fire
but succumbed last June

to Las Conchas fire.
For a while phantom
ashen logs hovered
where trees expired:

some upright, others
suspended midair. But winds
kicked up. Dense forest
razed. No ponderosas
left to reseed, reforest.

JORNADO DE MUERTO

Furtive traveler
beware a dead sea's
crystal meth sand.

Delirious night crossing:
sweat, saline tears,
lungs fill like a sack of ash.

If you trip—
don't stumble.
Invisible powdered

salt blinds the eyes.
Stick-cross marker,
choking stardust

blankets death's
legacy: White Sands
secret bomb site,

atomic hot spot,
humanity's
self-induced hell.

HOPE CHEST

Like itinerant sandhill cranes
comb the fields of Los Ranchos
looking for spilled seed,
a homeless woman picks

through rags in a garbage heap
gleaning secrets buried deep.
Colonies of mold sprout
at the edges of limp boxes.

White sheet a canvas of green
and red stains. Plastic—ugly,
cheap and indestructible—
thrives. Everything else rots,

even a decrepit hope chest
like the one she never filled
with embroidered pillow cases
and fancy linen napkins.

That old chest, a coffin
of memories, musty
baby clothes,
moth-chewed woolens.

Ragtag memories bear
witness to past lives,
the impermanence,
raw freight and salvage.

WHAT THE HOUSE COULDN'T HOLD

After the divorce Rachel
moved to a tiny house
by the tracks. Behind rotting
fence, horse-drawn plows

rusty from old sweat pocked
the track-scarred land.
What she couldn't toss she kept.
Not in the house, that

was crammed. *Put the rest
under the lanai*, she told movers.
Under fiberglass shelter
in brick-lined patio, bundles

of patched stained bedding,
carousel trays, faded slides.
Monopoly, Parchesi,
board games the kids

played sitting around
the dining room table
after dishes were cleared.
Months passed.

Pacific fog crept
under cover of night,
nourished brownish orange
patina on rusted trivets,

the iron skillet, old
metal rake. Heirlooms,
family photos, greeting cards,
moldered in metal drawers.

DEVIL'S BREATH

Wind-thrashed fire wall
sears mile-wide swath
down Cobb mountain.

Former writing cabin
a mound of cinders. Surreal
ash-powdered stone Buddha,

eyes gently shut,
sole survivor at Harbin springs.
Unqualified, devastating.

Worse fire, drought on record.
Scorching Devil's breath,
choking black haboobs,

obsidian ladened toxic fog
clogs cities. Clamp windows
tight. Silence swamp coolers.

Stay inside. Inhale
with your mouth shut.
Back east people sandbag

homes, blast levees
brimming with ornery, reckless
floods. Curse moisture's

incarnations: rain, hail,
sleet, snow while we
lust for a few muddled drops.

BONE BLACK

Early Sanskrit scribes
scraped dried soot
from oil lamps, charred
bones, to make rich
coal-black inks.

Carbon from scorched
pine tints my sumi ink stick.
Bison, horses and great black
bulls drawn in charcoal still
gallop across paleolithic
cave walls.

To think in fire's wake
there's something to salvage.
After death my burnt
pulverized bones might
tint some artist's palette.

ABOVE, BELOW GROUND

At Findhorn, utopian community
on the North Sea, people craft homes
from old whiskey stills. On hot days
curved womb-like walls emit faint
traces of oak-aged single malt.
Grasses sprout above sod roofs.

Wizened gardeners coax their crops,
whisper praises, gratitude.
Rutabagas, carrots, sown and reaped
by a lunar watch. Abundant supplies
for sale in the shop: whole grains,
tonics, supplements, honey,

bins of loose-leaf organic teas.
One afternoon in a village pub
ruby sun-flamed orbs pirouette
above glowing embers yet no visible
log burns."Peat from the bogs"
the waitress tells me. "Burns

for hours." Underground
primordial organic peat,
moldering swamp dung
harvested from a local bog
smolders, hidden like grief,
for days, months, centuries.

SMUDGE POT

Darjeeling tea steeps
in red floral teapot.
I fill monsoon teacup,
sip again brewed handpicked

leaves from Mim's tea estate.
Women pickers, barrel-sized baskets
strapped to their foreheads, waved
as I walked the road to Kalimpong,
small traveler's sack on my back.

Inky newsprint smudges
my fingertips.
As a girl in the orange
groves of Riverside
I pinched my nose
shut with one hand,

held the other against
potbellied outdoor chimney
that belched sooty smoke
to blanket orchards

before a frost. Orange
groves, smudge pots
long gone now.
Even the frost is rare.

FIVE

ANKLET

The one you bring
is heavy, Berber silver.
Metal grasps my ankle
like a shackle:

firm, unbending,
barely visible
under the cuff
of my blue jeans.

The anklet gently
chaffs my heel so
I walk differently.
Rhythmic, determined,
like a water buffalo,
you say, straining
towards some
watering hole.

At night by the light
of a pine scented candle
I enslave you with pallid
sphinx-like murmurings.

Cool metal tingles
your thigh like
rare breezes from
a palm leaf fan.

RIVER LIGHTS

Each fall Varanasi peddlers
stock hundreds of shallow
earthen cups so small
one easily fits in the palm

of my hand. People buy
dozens, fill with mustard oil,
twisted cotton wicks. At dusk
children light the Diwali

festival lamps. From the river
buildings rise up the banks,
illumined with diamonds,
flaming garlands.

Twinkling necklaces adorn
roof terraces. Blushing Ganga
temple spires ascend like rows
of tiered candles on church altars.

FIRE CEREMONY

Vedic mountain wedding
attendant stacks kindling
gleaned from hibiscus shrubs
and rhododendron trees.

Beside the outdoor pit
square like a prayer mat
offerings in small clay bowls.
Lotus peaked ridges rim

the valley like a vajra wall.
Cross-legged we sit atop
hand-loomed dragon carpet
carried by yak over high

mountain pass. The priest
hums an ancient prayer.
Pungent smoke from thirty-two
sacred flowers, herbs and grains

perfume the air like fine
incense. Petals of rose,
marigold, medicinal
herb flowers, sandalwood,

frankincense. Oils next,
sesame, coconut and ghee,
tease lusty flames. Small
brass ladle tips a medley

of wheat, barley and millet grains
over coals. Wafting smoky scent.
Demure, heavenly sky glow
above. Silver halo circles meek

winter sun, a witness ten thousand
miles from home. No best man,
bridesmaid, gown or tux.
At twenty-five I give myself away.

LUMINARIAS

After the fall equinox wafting smoke
from piñon fires. Hand-cranked
chili roasters thicken the chilled
air like gravy. Days traipse home,
weary sentinels on tired legs.

Sandhill cranes squawk,
circle high above shimmering
fall pinwheels, yellow
leaf spirals. Outback ground
squirrel pilfers green walnuts,

pecans. Lawn pocked where
he tunnels, dragging his loot up
to his mesa burrow that towers
over our land. A dry year only
a trickle in the ditch. Cottonwoods

don't complain. Their imminent
loss masked with dazzling array.
Sun on seasonal flame trees
ignites the bosque like luminarias
on Christmas eve.

WEEDS, TENDED OR NOT

In scruffy desert yard
wind/bird scattered seeds
sprout. La curandera
stalks herbs, cacti, roots, bark.

Her mind maps nature's
wild bounty. Every living
thing a miracle. Never curse
a weed. Many are useful:

yarrow for cramps or I Ching
throws. Harvest dew-glistened
leaves at dawn. Ferment
dandelion blooms for wine.

Sautè bitter amaranth.
Simmer mouth-puckering
sorrel. A rainless season
in the bosque. Weeds

thrive on dew and sweat,
suck up moisture
like ravenous leeches
impossible to pull off.

On the back roads
I scan open spaces,
forage wild edibles.
If shepherd's purse, dock

or lamb's quarters sprout
let them grow. Easier to harvest
what thrives naturally than
nurture seedlings from scratch.

TO KEEP THE COLD OUT

My windows brace
for the storm.
The horizon smothers
in flurries of white
and you boast, I'll keep

you warm, sliding
eel-like between sheets.
My nightgown is sheer.
Wood floor shivers
as I race from closet to bed.

The harder you grip me
the more snow I see.
Snow covers my desk,
fills the room,
settles over the city.

To think that water
can be so light, flake
by flake amassing a quiet
hold over things that move
in any way but down.

INVENTORY

The steam iron hisses
like a rattle snake,
scorches my shirt
when it overheats.

The toaster charred
bread to a crisp then
quit last Christmas.
You never bothered
with an electric shaver.

Frayed percolator cord
sparked, shocked if touched.
I could use a hair dryer
this winter and that washing
machine we never had.

But think of the energy
and money we're saving.
We're like two yogis
in a mountain cave
cooking nettle soup
on a campfire.

So what if they shut
off the power? Who
needs electricity?
It's summer. Honeysuckle
perfumes the yard.

If you get cold wrap
your arms around me.
Fire up the charcoal
hibachi. We'll barbecue.

Just bring your beer
chilled when you come
 home and don't expect
any ice cream sundaes.

HEAT WAVE

Fever clamors
like a rusty air conditioner,
gravel rattles my ears.
I can't turn it off.

Like the din of a crowded
city during a heat wave,
people take to the streets.
You can't shut them out.

An hourglass of tin
pebbles clanging down
the chute jars me from
some opium-laced relief.

Sleep is a whimper
clawing the door
or a saw-toothed *sadhu*
hobo tending the coals.

PERFECT RICE

Fearless rice woman
never measures. She knows
just when to cut the flame,
simmer to an airy fluff,
delicate cohesion of moist
grains. Her rice is never

gooey. Perfect rice eludes
me like crepe suzettes.
Globs stick to the pot
like pudding. In my mouth
rice turns to lumps
of uncooked dough.

So I abstain, renew
my vow. Hold out
for Chinese take-out.
A dream intrudes, visions
of dainty white mounds
in ivory porcelain bowls.

Imagine steamed basmati rice
and spicy *sag panir*,
spinach, and cheese curry.
Bolstered by a swig of sake,
a newfound recipe
in a ladies' magazine

—thirty minutes to a tantalizing
renaissance of rice—
I succumb, coax grains
into the pot, toss in words
of endearment and abide
by the rules like a nun.

COMPOST

Eons before I plotted
small twelve-by-twelve foot
veggie patch, lava cinder cone
beyond the yard shut down, dried up.

Who knows why. Was it abrupt
or the tail end of a slow volcanic
decline? Doug fir forest now cloaks
Rocky Butte. Red cedar needles mulch

the south side. My turf lower down
is baked ashen clay—back-wrenching
to dig—gritty, stubborn. I save the juiciest
kitchen scraps, fruits and veggies

to compost, make arable what is
hardscrabble. With pitchfork I fold
apple cores, pears, beets, potato skins
into the heap. Glistening oval papaya

seeds, bruised bananas, hairy kiwi rinds—
even a salmon's silvery scales to bury
deep. Till, mulch, water. Summer
crookneck squash leaves wide as elephant

ears canopied dark humus soil. Four
healthy volunteer tomato plants sprouted,
thrive even in that gentle shade.
Sun-flushed fruit, heavy on the vine.

76

SWALLOW

A handwritten note
slips out of a cookbook
on a pantry shelf.

My son's faded handwriting
on flimsy folded
blue airmail paper.

I'm getting better
at disguising that
familiar ache of grief.

What nourishes now
doesn't enter the mouth
but wells up from
a deep core.

SIX

TICKLERS

old Mayfield School, Palo Alto

Twice a day when the recess bell
clamored on the cracked wall
kids raced through the echoing
corridor, spilled down cement ramp.

First one out yelled, "I won!"
If I fell both knees scraped and bled;
tender skin scabbed for weeks.
Too bad girls couldn't wear jeans.

We'd run so much faster, slide into
second or third base—even score
a few home runs—impossible
in those flimsy gathered cotton skirts.

But skirts weren't all bad. To twirl
and twirl on the grassy field dizzied,
my head circled like a carousel.
The ground rose to the sky where

Chinatown dragons and covered
wagons chugged aimlessly across
the lofty blue expanse before
morphing into eels or, once, a go-cart.

School somersaulted upside down as I
hung by my knees from the cross-bars.

Long braids swept the sandbox. *I see
London, I see France...* Twenty daisies,

asters really, what the yard worker
called weeds, I wove into a lei
for the Maypole dance. I sucked wild
licorice anise stalks from a wayside bush

that forged a life between sidewalk
cracks in the parking strip off
College. Wedge a thick blade
of Bermuda grass between thumbs

to make a squeaker, then blow
your lungs out. Kiss tag or spin
the bottle behind the bike shed.
When the boys split into teams,

played further downfield, girls met
secretly behind the backstop. On a dare
we pulled our panties down
to our knees then whirled like dervishes

in the slim shadows. Full skirts bellowed,
breezes whipped goose-bumped thighs
like feather ticklers from the party
aisle at Woolworth's Five & Dime.

POET'S COUCH

Spring cleaning at the bookstore
begins after New Year. Books crowd
walls, tables, cupboards and closets.
There are never enough shelves.
What can't fit on shelves towers off the floor.

We look around. Where to add
shelves? Fiction, poetry, Southwest
and art sections all need more space.
Even the kitchen's crammed with cookbooks.
At monthly readings poets clutch

books, briefcases, harmonicas, coffee
mugs, cell phones, note books and glasses
then settle on the old navy couch by the window.
"The couch!" we exclaim in unison.
"We'll move the couch to add new shelves!"

Reluctantly we load the cumbersome
thing upright onto a wheeled cart to
maneuver between boxes in the narrow aisle.
Out on the street a large FREE sign
beckons drivers on a sleepy Saturday

morning on 4th Street, the old Route 66.
Traffic is slow but steady. Anyone need a couch?
A poet's couch? Within the hour a beat-up
Cadillac rumbles to the curb. A man shifts
to park then idles the engine while a woman

steps out, leans back into navy foam cushions
imagining perhaps stretching out for an afternoon
nap or crocheting a woolen scarf while
balancing a bowl of posole or minestrone
on a TV tray. She nods her approval.

But a Cadillac is no pick-up. How…!
Without speaking they lift in unison, slide
one end of the couch onto the back bumper
then shove. Up, up and over the rear
window until it rests atop the vehicle

like a canoe above a duck hunter's car.
They didn't bring rope. Never mind!
The car waits for a clearing then creeps
into traffic. The driver, mindful of the teetering
load, eases over a speed bump.

Later that night after the couple slinks
off to the warmth of their bed voices
may slowly rise from the depths
of the couch like spirits on All Soul's Night.
We heard them. Softly at first, barely

audible whisperings echo through walls.
Strains of Dickinson, Sexton and Plath
filter under doors, pillows. Dreaming
minds mouth words of longing,
the soul's mysterious cravings.

BLUE ALCHEMY

At the paint store to pick a new color
for the kitchen, something fresh, vibrant.
"What about blue?" I say remembering

cowering glacier in last night's dream.
"Not Turquoise or Baby Blue. Indigo
is too dark, Cobalt too heavy."

Color chart names leap off the counter
conjuring places, dredging memories.
Not the Lapis of a lover's gift idling in

jewelry box with broken clasp. No blue
veins, hypothermic lips or bruises.
No blue tracks, blood, shoes or moon.

We didn't find Blue Lake, sacred Taos
watershed or Blue Hole's desert oasis.
No delicate robin's egg, no ribbons,

blue stockings, jeans or collars.
How about an ancient Oceanic Blue,
Teal, Cerulean or Royal Blue?

"Let's cook under Mediterranean
Blue," I say, "the blue of morning
mists: Nautilus, Neptune's Breath."

Our kitchen galley will float like an
Aegean ship: Mariner, Aquamarine,
peacock, jay, kingfisher.

When I close my eyes: Istanbul's
tiled Blue Mosque, Vishnu's ghostly tint
and Shiva's blue poison-filled throat.

The hardest choice comes last, earthly heavens:
divine blue of a Virgin's robe, Blue Rapture,
Celestial Blue or just plain Wondrous.

LIVE FROM THE UPTOWN

To jazz up decrepit, abandoned
department store we dragged up wood
panels from two floors down,
built a bar where Woodstock kids
once bought cub scout uniforms.

Recycled blue velvet theater curtain
draped the stage, rows of cast iron
refurbished theater seats, exposed brick
walls. The Uptown was totally
hands on, a Do It Yourself nightclub.

Booker, bouncer, publicist and sound
guy—that was Gary after working
the bookstore next door ten to five.
I tended bar, hosted art crawls,
readings and wine tastings.

Guinness, Sam Adams on tap,
chilled Duval and pilsner Urquell.
Bowls of salt peanuts, wafting aroma
of chocolate chip cookies fueled
intermission crowds. Once before

a show Dave Burrell flat on his back
under the Baldwin. "Man!
What happened?" "It's cool.
I'm connecting." Later he banged
those keys so hard three clanked

to the floor. That baby grand took
loads of abuse, kept tuner John busy
on emergency post-concert runs.
One player propped the lid open,
yanked, hammered tender strings

with crude wood mallets. Hot Tuna's
Harvey Sorgen showed up sans drums
after late-night gig, threw black
leather jacket over chair seat
to jam on stage. Giardullo put us

on the Free Jazz circuit. Standing room
only for Dewey. Teri conjured the
sweetest sugar cakes then blew
us away on The A Train. Other nights
Fathead, Joe Lovano, Don Byron

drove upriver or down off
the mountain to sit, listen in.
During a blizzard vocalist
Laurel Massé's fans couldn't get
out of their driveways. Six of us

clapped so loud if you tuned
in her WBAI show that night
you'd swear she had a house full
of die-hards. Live from the Uptown!
How sweet that sounds.

ABOUT THE AUTHOR

Marilyn Stablein is the author of fifteen books. She won the New Mexico Book Award, the National Federation of Press Women Book Award, a Southwest Writers Award, and was a finalist for the Marie Alexander Prose Poetry Award.

Her books include *Splitting Hard Ground: Poems*; *Houseboat on the Ganges & A Room in Kathmandu*; *Sleeping in Caves*; a collection of eco-essays set in the northwest, *Climate of Extremes: Landscape and Imagination*; and *Vermin: A Traveler's Bestiary*. *The Census Taker: Tales of a Traveler in India and Nepal* won publication, writing and design awards.

Former book critic for *The Seattle Times* and founding board member of Seattle Arts and Lectures, Ms. Stablein received Creative Writing degrees from the University of Washington and the University of Houston. Her writing and illustrations are widely published in magazines, journals, books and anthologies. Her limited-edition artist books are in private and public collections. She is based in Portland, Oregon.

Visit: marilynstablein.com